MORGAN ELLIA SHERIDAN

Morgan Sheridan was very young when she started writing poetry and throughout her life, it has always been the true manuscript of her emotions.

Morgan grew up on the south coast of England, UK, she spent much of her misspent youth by the sea, writing poetry at a bus stop, waiting for the number 8 bus to her destiny.

Her father was in the military and her mother was a Jehovah's Witness. She lived her life in the fast lane, being a hedonist, doing everything she could to hide her addictions and mental illness.

Morgan moved to London and studied Acting and Music at Rose Bruford Drama School and has worked in television, film and radio. She now prefers a tranquil and not-so-crazy life in Guildford, Surrey.

This introductory selection of her works, takes you on a visceral and intimate journey.

Her words are a sensitive marriage, of evocative pictures and insightful observation of the paradoxical beauty and irony of everyday life.

INTERNAL ANGLES

Poetry by Morgan Sheridan

©2024 Morgan Ellia Sheridan. All rights reserved.

Morgan Ellia Sheridan has asserted her right to be identified as the author of this publication in accordance with the Copyright, Designs and Patents Act 1988. All rights reserved. No part of this publication may be reproduced, stored in a retrieval system, or transmitted in any form or by any means, electronic, mechanical, photocopying, recording or otherwise, without the prior permission of the copyright owner.

ISBN 978-1-80439-504-2

A CIP catalogue record for this book is available from the British Library
Artwork by Phil Armstrong Creative: philarmstrong.com
Images used under license from Shutterstock.com

DEDICATION

Great thanks to:

Chanelle, Phil, Russ, Emma, Jane, Stretchly, Katie & Simon,
Jessie, Sue, Becky, and especially Scottish Roy.
Georgie my hairy son, I miss you.

All those who had faith and belief in me and my work.

The universe at large and the powers that be,
that work in ways beyond my understanding.

The world, for teaching me lessons in life.
If it wasn't for those experiences,
my words would mean nothing.

P.S. Martin, 'Millwall doesn't suck!'

CONTENTS

ORDINARY-GIRL	7
GOING OUT BAG	9
VICIOUS CIRCLE	10
IMPOSSIBLE DREAM	12
THE BOOK OF MY HEART	14
QUIET PLACE TO CRY	17
CALM	18
RACHEL	21
SILENCE	23
LOOKING IN	25
TEN MORE MINUTES	26
THE REPLY	29
PLASTIC CHAIRS	30
BROKEN EGG	32
MILLENNIALS	35
THIS SPACE	36
STILL BURNING	39
CONCRETE STARE	40
CASUAL SMILE	43
ENERGY	45
LOVE STAND	46
KISS	48
MORE	50
LATE	53
BLAH!	55
NOTHING THE SAME	57
OEUF	58
OEUF	59
LOVE'S LATENCY	61
A PLACE TO BELONG	62
QUIET SOLACE	65
THE PERFECT CADENCE	66
PAIL FULL OF SORROW	69
NEAR TO ME	70
TRISTE RICHE	72
THE NEW YEAR'S SONG	75
TAIL PLIGHT	76
STILLNESS	79
SAD I	81
XMAS NEXTMASS	82
X-Y	84
SYNC	87
APRIL SHOWERS	88
I AM THE UNIVERSE IN ME	91
BONSAI OF WORDS	92
I HAVE NO ANSWERS	94
COMMUTING MACHINE	97
MUSIC IS	98
START AGAIN	100
WAITING	102
TREASURE BOX	104
I AM MY DREAMS	107
TOLERANCE	109
A YEAR	110

BACK CONTENTS NEXT

ORDINARY-GIRL

Ordinary-girl.
Wouldn't look twice in a crowded room.
Look over your glass and look again,
She's gone.
You stare in awe,
But that's not what I am for.

Ordinary-girl.
Average statistics.
About right, about nice.
But the glamour bus, I missed it.
Fell asleep.
Hung over on the night bus to fame.
Got stoned when I got there,
And got soaked in the rain.

Ordinary-girl.
Toying with Twitter, but nothing to say.
Lost track of my soapbox.
Trashed it, somewhere in my rebellious youth.
Writing nothing,
Still trying to find my truth.

GOING OUT BAG

Crumpled in a corner,
Contents strewn across the table.
Every fag burn, tells a story,
Every stain, a morning glory.

And it's got the same old shit, lighter and lipstick.
Same old lines, ragged round the edges,
Pulled its way through hedges,
With the same old shit, lighter and lipstick.

And it always finds its way home,
And it never asks questions, tactful suggestions.

A silent provider.
A closet insider.

Another night on the tiles,
High heels and painful smiles.
Clutching the same old shit, lighter and lipstick.
Hailing a cab, vaping, no fag.

A zillion messages on my phone.
Relieved but messy,
I crawl home.
Still with the same old shit, lighter and lipstick.

Rain check on the shag.
My going out bag.

VICIOUS CIRCLE

Got to earn.

Got to work.

To pay, to live,
To eat, to survive.

Need a job.
To serve.
To give, to live,
To eat, to survive.

Need to study.
To learn.
To do, to work,
To earn, to pay,
To live, to survive.

Need to pay.

To study.
To learn, to do,
To work, to earn,
To pay, to survive.

Need a job.

To pay.
To study, to learn,
To do, to earn,
To live, to survive.

Got to earn...

IMPOSSIBLE DREAM

Why can't I manage to write right?
I'm totally wasted,
But should be inspired.
Wired,
On edge,
On a ledge,
Underfed,
Starved of ideas,
Fears,
Tears,
From years of abuse.
Mental overuse.

Now I'm stronger.
Not younger,
Older,
And colder.
In a place,
Welded with solder.
Confidence closet,
Fear,
Squeezes, like a corset.

But still…

I go on.
Afraid to do wrong,
But it's all for the song,
For the impossible dream.
Letting off steam,
Embrace the child in me,
For all to see.
Let one light see the light,
And never retreat.
Never back down,
Or fear to write.

Time to take flight,
Escape from the page,
Taste all the rage,
And be free,
Once and for all.
And it's bigger than me,
And it's gestated too long.
It's well overdue.

And you…

Can you rear this child?
This universal creation?
That needs two hearts to make it so.
Mine are the words,
Your knowledge makes them grow.
Be the greenhouse for these dreams?
Somewhere safe,
Where sunshine gleams?

There is a reason,
There is a season,
Born at the right time,
Scurvy to lime.

Inspired,
Desired,
Ignited,
Re-fired,
Head out of the sand,
Finding courage in your hand.

And now…

Two quiet dreamers,
Hug trees in the moonlight,
Out of sight,
Above love,
More than we see.
This is sitting,
Behind your own eyes.
And seeing,
Something far bigger,
Than we.

For the impossible dream,
Your wings make me fly.
Now I'm stronger,
Bolder, older,
Wiser in years,
Outgrown my peers,
Ink fills my page,
Ideas flow like a stream,
I am living,
My impossible dream.

IM~~POSSIBLE~~

INTERNAL ANGLES 15

THE BOOK OF MY HEART

The book of my heart,
Is loose-leafed.
The pages fall out,
Scatter like rain,
Illegal like cocaine,
Yet buzzy when you're down.
Miss it, when it's not around.

The book of my heart,
Is in a foreign tongue,
And doesn't always make sense.
It spits when it's hurt,
Face down in the dirt,
Doesn't see wood, just trees,
But all gnarled,
And crooked with disease.

The book of my heart,
Waffles a lot.
But never says what it means.
Too afraid to say,
Always walks away,
A bit too mixed up and verbose.
Paranoid overdose.

The book of my heart,
Is never read.
Always goes back on the shelf,
Dostoevsky of my soul,
Too big, for a pigeon hole.
Thinks always the worst,
Hides that fear, in verse.

The book of my heart,
Is yours to dissect.
Naked and uncensored,
Fragile and weak,
Nonconformist, oblique.
Shakespeare on speed,
But worth a read.

BACK CONTENTS NEXT

QUIET PLACE TO CRY

I searched and could not find,
A quiet place to clear my mind.
Distant I travelled, from the angular sky,
To find a quiet place to cry.

Far far away from the madding crowd,
I ventured to find silence in a bitter shroud.
My heart kept post like a foreign spy,
None could enter to hear my sigh.

A quiet place to cry,
Betwixt and between the earth and sky.
But I could not find, a place to stand,
For millions stood, the same as I.

CALM

At peace,
Silent release,
Dusty corridors left alone,
A feather, cast in a sea breeze.
Torrid valleys I have clambered,
Jagged pieces of disjointed forgetting.
And now I remember.
I cast my line in and drag out the ghosts.

Back again to the silent corridors.
Chasms in any hollow,
Spaces in any hiding place,
Where there is so much internal infinity,
Yet the walls are silent as death.

Calm…

Where once the screams tore the skirting.
And curled like smoky fingers,
Round the fittings.
The dust drifts out on the duster flag,
Fluttering out of the window,
Taken by the breeze.

There is light again in the silent corridors.
Chastised places,
Constantly chased by faces,
Invisible as a lover's kiss.
Forever etched in ink and wood,
Memories are swept up with the broom,
A small, dark, box, room.

Calm…

That's where I used to go,
My special place.
Calm,
And warm,
Hidden from the fray,
Safe for a day.

Strange lonely girl.
But I was never lonely to me.

INTERNAL ANGLES 21

RACHEL

Rachel.
Old Rachel,
Wise Rachel,
Were you right?
Did you see, what was out of sight?

Green-haired hippie,
Or converter of the weak?
Did you know?
Did you suspect?
These secrets, that I seek?

I sought them then.
In my visions,
In my sleep,
I'd beseech.
But they were so far out of reach.

Rachel.
Old Rachel,
Part of my past,
I cannot see,
You're still so much,
A part of me.

I love you, but you don't think of me,
If you're still alive at all.
The smell of the thick pile rug,
And the untouchable ornament shelf.

You'll never see,
What I will be,
If that BE,
Is anything at all.
And even then,
You won't ooze praise.
Just a silent condemnation,
From an older generation.

Tonight is for you,
The one I loved.
Old wise Rachel.

SILENCE

Silence is golden.
My family should be millionaires.
Subtext in JavaScript,
You have to join nerds anonymous,
To get a translation.

The more the wind blows,
The emptier they seem.
Dysfunctional bunch of lone atoms,
Bombing around,
Stating just the obvious.

It's oh so status quo,
Oh so contained and distant.
I know more about strangers,
Endless rooms full of elephants,
Disquieting thoughts, quietly sizzling.

Silence is pc,
Silence is agreed,
Silence is written,
It's the lines between, you read.

BACK CONTENTS NEXT

LOOKING IN

She withdrew into herself.
First writing for one,
For the reasons,
As we all do,
Searching for answers.
Thinking it was not becoming,
For others to read,
To pry, to know,
To decide, or judge.
Who would relate,
Just berate.
What's the point, it's just the past.
Who cares to read?
What difference would it make?
To pick apart, each mistake.

But then,
Sat with my words,
Engrossed in their pain.
Someone was touched,
knowing we're all the same.
In this world full of solitary,
Through her tortoise rims,
Eyes belie years of knowing,
Behind those brims.

Light and dark, are the same.
She looked through my soul,
And back again.

So I shuffled away,
Heart in a pile of loose-leafed script.
And the story begins.

First out of company.
To imagine the world.
Internal angles,
Fractals of isolated prisms,
Twisting by hurt,
Reforming by learning,
Ever changing,
Like life.

Patient like the sun.
Wise and silent, like the sea.
Whose waves, calmed an open mind,
Expanded a willing watcher.
Looking for the stone with a hole,
A space for a soul,
A place for her dreams,
Universal slipstreams.

And she found it right there,
In the years she watched,
but never saw.
Forever looking out,
For the ship that never came,
Saw the half-empty glass,
As more of the same.

But words flowed here,
And the angels sat and spoke.
Her higher self of knowing,
Effortless like the ocean flowing.
Deep and ancient, in those moments,
Breathing in the tide and times,
Looking out through wiser eyes.
And always saw the world this way,
But never knew until today,
When the eyes that were always open,
Through tortoise rims,
Started,
Looking,
In.

TEN MORE MINUTES

As I leave, the train is delayed.
Ten more minutes to think,
Of me.
Who I am, where I'm going?

Nine more minutes to consider,
How do you feel?
What do you want?

Eight more minutes,
And the clock strikes each day off the list.

Seven more minutes to imagine,
A thousand other visions,
On these electrified tracks of thought.

Six more minutes and the freeze-frame,
Holds up eternity in an eight by ten.

Five more minutes till I distance myself from your smile.

Four more minutes and life will turn into normality again,
And you will forget my name.

Three more minutes and I imagine you here,
To say goodbye.
And all the other words,
That could fill my impatient vacuum.

Two more minutes and the air is filled,
With trundling wheels and squeaky cases.

The train leaves a minute earlier than expected.
I reserved that last minute for you.

Now that's gone too.

INTERNAL ANGL

THE REPLY

I sent.
But now it's not what I meant!
I mean... not what I said,
But what you read.
It wasn't quite the way to...
Did I want to say.
I don't quite know,
But it wasn't what I know,
You thought I meant.

They are me.
They scared you away.
Not that I wanted you, in that way.
You expected more, I wanted less,
Now you digress,
And think me strange,
When that wasn't my intention,
Now that you mention,
Months later.
Like it traumatised your conscience.
When that wasn't what I meant at all.

At least you read them.
That's all I wanted really,
Someone to say nearly,
They could comprehend their meaning.
Not with any judgement.
I'm not a case for incarceration,
These pages are just a gestation,
For objective inner thoughts to come,
If they weren't so close, to make you run.

Who could read,
But not see the pictures.
And live the memories,
But not feel the twitches.
These words created,
At least you read them.
But you've made it into a drama,
To the wolves you fed them.

But it was never meant to be,
Scales fall, and now I see.
Because of the content,
The space well spent.
On ejecting emotion,
Misdirected devotion.

And it really wasn't,
What I meant at all.

PLASTIC CHAIRS

Plastic chairs.
Some that spin,
Some that stand,
Some that curve,
Some just sit.

Plastic chairs.
Temporary comfort,
In a transient environment.
Bland and empty,
Void and numb.

Gone is the status,
From bench to throne.
Uniform.
Surrounded by rows,
Of sameness.

Plastic chairs.
Our stop and go,
Chop and change world.
Where nothing lasts,
Past four and twenty.

Moulded by the million,
Elastic, plastic,
Frenetic, pathetic,
Conducive sedation,
Statement of a generation,
Plastic chairs.

BROKEN EGG

The broken egg.
The broken frame.
That holds up the frail,
Replaced, not repaired,
When it starts to fail.

Assumed ever present.
Overlooked ever resident.
Gnarled sticks, curl over the top,
Weathered slippers,
Cover darned socks.

But what can it be?
And where can it go?
It's for a transition,
A temporary position.

To heal, then discarded,
Or support the retarded.
Sounds so hard, so harsh,
But true.
I am only useful to you.
For a while, for support,
Until you are taught,
By courage,
To stand alone.

So much I have seen,
Tested the mean.
An epic, in a grain of sand,
The future, written in your hand.

And when I was no use to you,
When you sent me away.
I had no place to stay.
No use in that state,
Shattered like a plate,
All broken and mislaid.
The frame needs to be, re-sprayed.

But there was no glue, no tape,
No helping hand,
No quick escape.
No fix and replace,
Just an empty room.

With a half-made bed,
I broke like an egg.

A broken egg.
All splayed out on the floor.
No corners to hold me, anymore.
Shed from my casing,
In line for erasing.

And I wondered at the lessons to learn,
And stared, into the space of silence…
And everything burned.
Because I failed the test,
And laid 'us' to rest.
I broke at the off,
When you needed me so bad,
You were all I ever had.
When I had to be your world,
I felt like a weakling girl.
Not strong, like a man.

And now, I hold your hand.
So slight and weak…
I give all the energy I have,
In the words we don't speak.
And it hurts, when I hear your name,
But it's only you, that cures your pain.
When I feel a head-rush, from the drain,
And pains within, I can't explain
I feel so ill prepared,
To be your walking frame.

It is always the carers that are mistook.
Overlooked.
That juggle to support the weak,
And there is no carer, for a carer to seek.
When a counsellor is in need of an ear,
People just assume, he is there to hear.
And heal, that's the deal.
But it's not resent,
Because your love is heaven sent.
And I give my heart, with all my will,
And I'd give my world, to not have you ill.
But by my side,
In whose trust, I confide.

But it's when your tongue cuts me down,
Egg is broken all around.
Your energy sucks me dry,
Then you poke me in the eye.
With your dismissive tone,
And your ever critical zone.

Then there's a stain,
I am the egg again.

Left rotting, on the kitchen floor.
Bloodletting, behind the bathroom door.
Because love loses the bitter shell,
And love only grows,
When you kiss and tell.

But such a fragile frame,
Is so easily broken.
An egg is destroyed,
By harsh words,
Softly spoken.

But if Humpty can,
There's hope for us all.
I am living proof,
There is time to restore.

A broken egg,
Is broke no more.

INTERNAL ANGLES 35

MILLENNIALS

Across a sea of glass,
Etched existence and a silver pin curl.
The hopes she entertained,
Rustle in the bottom of her Sainsbury's bag.
Stone Age art sprawled across the skyline,
'Charmaine's sister's a slag'
And 'Millwall sucks'.

Grey is the silver glitz,
When the glitz wears away.
When the tin can clearers,
Sweep up the memories.
And the flickers of ash,
Land on the dying ashen trees.

Motto of our generation,
The millennials.

Next generation of the next generation,
Same generation as the muddled one before.
Next transmutation, of a twisted permutation,
That never got the problems solved,
In the chance they had before.

Forward-looking, future booking,
Faster, fairer, greyer, squarer.
A brief salutation, to a messed-up generation.
That didn't seem to sort it out,
In the chance they had before.

We were the crazy makers, the risk takers,
The children of the New Age baby makers.
We were meant to save the whale,
We were meant to tip the scale,
We were meant be the reference,
But instead we reek of indifference.

Motto of our generation,
The millennials.

Next generation of the next generation,
Same generation as the muddled one before.
Next transmutation, of a twisted permutation,
That never got the problems solved,
In the chance they had before.

Born under a bad sign, resigned, future is undefined.
He leaves disgrace at the door,
And his conscience on the floor.
Because he reasons, well it's not mine.
No one needs to own a home,
Coz everyone lives on their mobile phone.

Next generation of the next generation,
Clones of the order.
Come back when you're older.
To the land with no trees,
And flickers of regret.
Mindless mind set.

Generation of fools?
Millennials.

In no years' time, it's 2024,
We churn out the excuses, and wait for the draw.
What happened to the class of '99?
Did we get messed up on a night bus
Oh God, is that the time?

Across a sea of glass,
Testament to our existence in ice cores.
She spills her drink, 'Millwall scores!'
Statutory routine suspends in chores.
Her mind is in the comfort, of the void,
If stone is our only lasting legacy,
Lessons will be destroyed.
But Millwall will forever suck.

Motto of our generation,
The Millennials.

THIS SPACE

This space between now and later,
Seems like a decade.
Now there is a space, in my head, in my bed,
There are words that remain unsaid.
The space was not there before,
In all the times busily keeping score.
Hell bent on paying the rent,
And living the dreams,
That are fraying at the seams.

This space, is a product of your excursion,
It's a new version.
Of the reality, I was so comfy living.
Through the dirt, I was just sieving,
For gold nuggets of love, amongst the rubble.
You came along, labelled 'here comes trouble'.
And then you leave my arms, your charms,
Leave a vacant space in my heart,
And I'm wrenched apart.

By this new space, in between.
This space, unseen.
In my soul, there is a hole, in my bucket,
And once, I'd have said 'STUFF IT!'...

But this space, won't go away.
Where you lay,
Seems like where you belong?
Am I wrong?
Too long, for my heart, to go on?
The space, between now and later.
Empty and void,
Filled with empty noise.
Just a rustling of sheets,
And slow, aching, heartbeats.

Later, is when you return,
Later, is when we feel the burn.
Of two bodies burnt into one,
Two souls creating a sun.
Our bed is where stars are born,
Creating heaven, from a universe torn.
In this space of dark matter,
We move like the latter,
Stargazers, love grazers,
Dancing with lasers.

This space, is filled with lust,
From matter to dust.
Guilt erodes like rust,
Eating at our core,
But we still yearn for more.
Because this space we've created, is saturated,
With our dreams, with our desires,
With our hopes, as high as spires.

This space is more than just a bed,
This space is not just in my head.
This space has wings, if we both try,
To be the reason, for our why.

This space, was never there before,
And now I am left, wanting more.
Yearning for later, to be now,
Yearning that fate, will somehow,
Throw us a bone, give us a home,
A place to grow strong,
Finally, a place to belong.

INTERNAL ANGLES 39

BACK CONTENTS NEXT

STILL BURNING

Late again.
Age-old story,
Laid naked alone,
In all my glory.
No call, to say I'm late,
For another date.
Sorry you had to wait,
Around all evening,
Get my meaning?
Feel so confused,
And so used,
Where are you?

The candles burn.
They're still burning.
The Mozart plays,
The steam rises,
From my overactive thoughts,
It's only my heart that burns.

It's late, it's cold.
Whatever's left,
Is covered in mould.
I scrape off, my painted eyes,
And wipe away the tear-stained gutter lines,
That criss-cross my face,
And hide my disgrace.
It's no more, even before it's begun,
This silence has broken, my trust of one.

Broken my heart.
That exploding feeling,
When loving was never a chore.
No more.
The candles are still burning?
What am I still holding out for?
The finality of lingering waxen smoke,
There is no punchline for this joke.
As the candles end of their own accord,
I still listen for the door,
But the memory's stored.

Still burning...

CONCRETE STARE

Watch the street,
Just the street,
The smooth concrete.
Follow the gaze,
Amongst the smoggy urban haze.
This conveyer belt world,
Of lukewarm indifference.

This expansive empty personal space,
Buzzing with electrons and protons.
No need to touch,
Incarcerated in a world of solitary.
We offer our hand to science,
The god of all solutions,
The upholder of the impersonal and efficient.

Big brother is watching you,
In your car, on the street.
He's on the wall,
He's under your feet.
Function, as part of the machine,
Do not try to intervene,
All expression is obscene.

Watch the street,
Just the street,
The smooth concrete.
Follow the gaze,
Amongst the smoggy urban haze.
This conveyer belt world,
Of lukewarm indifference.

The concrete stare.

CASUAL SMILE

I was looking, but only with a casual smile.
A passing phase, a drunken daze.
I was looking, but my heart was full of lead.
Couldn't bring myself again to share my bed.
How you crept into my soul, I'll never know,
But there you are, and aboard you stowed.
A passenger on my path,
Here for a ride, up for a laugh.
I didn't really think much past,
A casual lay, a friend for a day.

But here we are,
Holding onto the same star.
Riding the same path,
And I love, more than just your laugh.
And I bathe in your smile,
Your lips linger, for more than a while.
And my passion stirs, the lust occurs,
I melt into your arms,
I am at the mercy of your charms.
And I beg for you inside, I have no place to hide,
Aching desire, passion's fire.
I explode in orgasmic bliss,
Tell me, how could one kiss, turn to this?

Who can tell, who can say?
I know only that, on that day,
I was looking, but only with a casual smile.
And somehow you stayed, more than a while.
So now my only wish, is this,
That you give this casual smile,
A dreamer's kiss.
And I pray that past, our drunken daze,
This love divine, is no passing phase.
I pray now that, you stay a while,
And this is more, than just, a casual smile.

ENERGY

It took me an age to understand,
This is external learning.
You are not, what I had planned,
Yet you are part of this brew.
Because a new me is fermenting.
All bottled up inside,
Corked up, time's up,
Parched dry, small fry,
Brimming with lamenting.

A new me is fermenting.

I see the energy swirl in you,
Exchange, rearrange,
And I came through.
Tired out, burnt out, washed up,
You drained my cup,
And I complain? Insane?
You seep like osmosis,
Through my membrane of light,
Somethin' ain't right?

It took me time to comprehend,
This internal churning.
That seemed to have no end,
Yet you are part of this view.
Because my nature is dissenting,
Free and wild,
Fired up, lighters up,
Mile high, do or die,
Overflowing, no repenting.

A new me is fermenting.

Stop draining me, of my energy.
But it's not you, in reality,
It's only me.
Your love doesn't twist my arm?
Or mean me harm?
I'm the sink?
I'm the one to think?

The world is an energy exchange.
We try to connect, like lucky slots,
With loose change.
We throw our pennies, gamble our chips,
You are seduced then shot down,
By deadly lips.
The tide tips, tempting hips,
Yet you are still part of this mix.
Quick fried, freeze dried,
Messed up, outta luck,
Raw inside, no need to hide.
Mystics reveal, now I see,
Energy, you are me.
I'm finally done, with resenting.

A new me, is fermenting.

LOVE STAND

I love you.
And no mountain can stop me.
All the bells can chime the hour,
But none can peal in my tower.
Lest they play to our tune,
This rune.
This riddle I can't explain,
My heart is yours to entertain.
And I am lost without you.

I love you.
And I know this is love.
And in this moment I am complete,
In this moment I feel release.
Struck between light and shade,
Light refracts but will not fade,
Tarnished with time,
But not yet jaded.
Look at our love stand,
We parade unaided.

I love you.
You inspire me to new heights.
Two kites,
Flying in the azure sky.
High, on a wind of change,
That blows from the west.
Love that will stand the test,
Of time.

KISS

First kiss was frightening, over like lightning.
Second kiss was testing,
Who knows what you're getting.
Third kiss was mature, but can't tell for sure.
Fourth kiss was shame, cut under fame.
Fifth kiss was a lark, a shot in the dark.
Sixth kiss was heaven, lasted eleven.
Seventh kiss was lies, my how time flies.
Eighth kiss was goodbye, tears and all cry.
Ninth kiss was forgiven, warm but forbidden.
Tenth kiss still lingering…
Eleventh kiss still remembering…
Twelfth kiss, last count, still revelling…

MORE

Each day I will venture,
To be a little bolder.

A little surer.

A little more.

Than I was before.

Being brave enough,
To just,
Be.

To take life by the horns,
And see.
To unveil my ghosts,
Then set them free.

Not scared to be alone.

Not clinging,
Fearing being disowned.
Breathing in the strength of one.
Now at last my time,
Has come.

INTERNAL ANGLES 53

LATE

The thunder and rain, the warm summer shower.
Midnight and moon shines,
Scattered rays like the headlights,
Distant sounds of a nervous whistle.

Head bowed low,
Scuttles across the street like a woodlouse.
Pitter-patters rushing, from the overflowing gutters,
Fast lanes which bubble, from an old fairy liquid bottle.

The clock ticks away seconds of life,
The sound deafens the silence.
The cord is still, the receiver silent,
But for the repetitive drone.
Un-vented frustration is taken out on an old sock.
Uncertainty hovers like an expectant father.
The receiver clicks down like a torrent of ash and cinder,
The remains of a beacon of hope in a dark land.

Emptiness fills the soul,
Takes its toll.
Apprehension takes the earth from our feet,
Be discreet.
We hope for a bridge, to cross our river of despair,
Someone to be there.

The thunder and rain, the warm summer shower.
After midnight, life crawls from its hovel.
Brushes off the telling stain,
Sliding under the window pane.
Bouncing a whistle off the half-lit streets,
Head bowed low, hoping no one will know.
The creeping door cries an apology,
To the eyes buried in a cushion,
On the sofa that waits for no man.

Late.

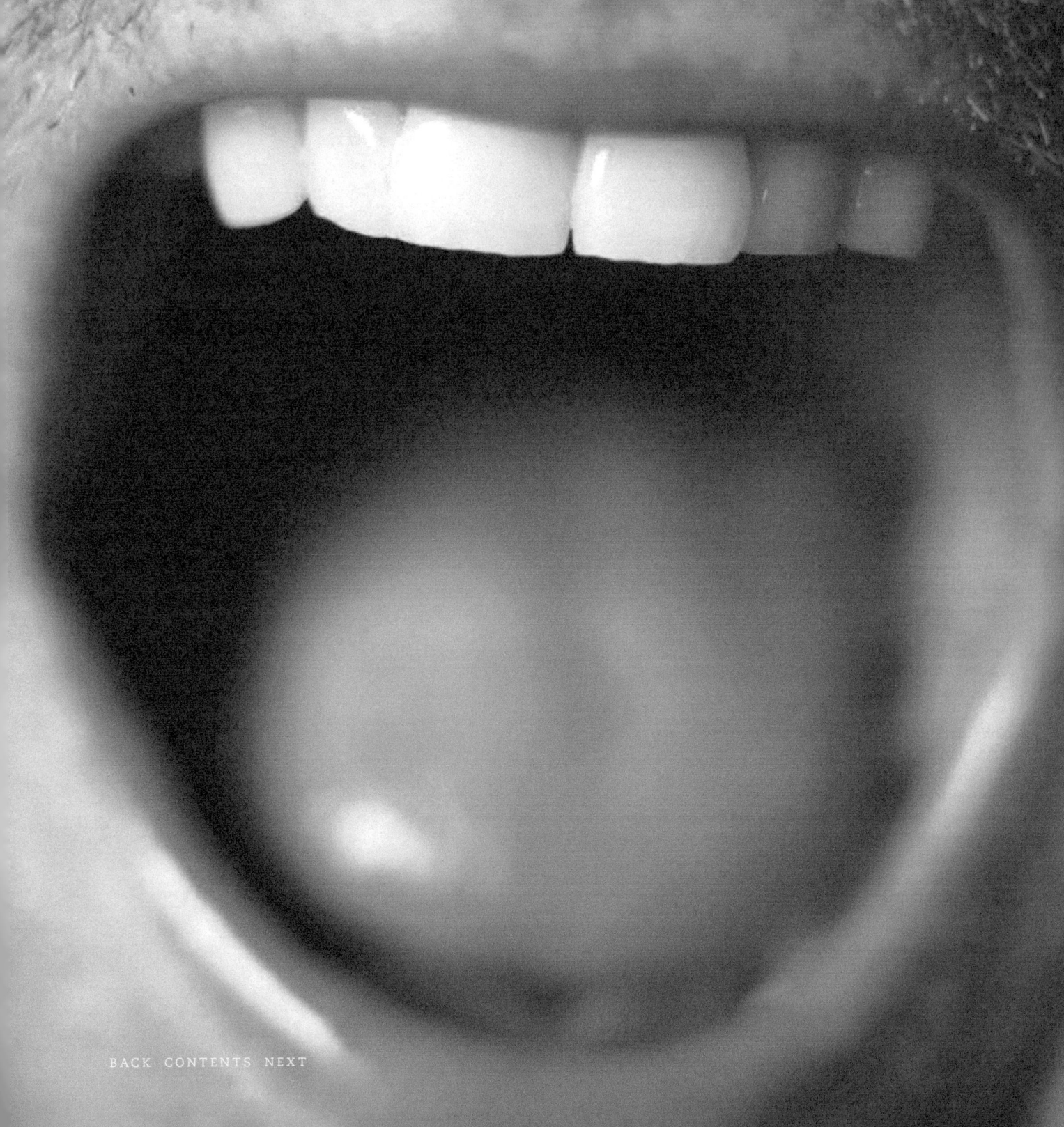

BACK CONTENTS NEXT

BLAH!

What! another?
Surely not?
Must be delusion.
No, it's intrusion.
Close, not an illusion.
Small and rectangle,
Quiet, silence then...

BLAH!

Out it comes!
In your face,
Fills the space,
Prepare to brace.
Buzzing like bees,
Look at my knees,
Fizzing with words,
Singing in thirds.
Connecting like electricity,
An energy,
That explodes in me,
Then...

BLAH!

Inspiration sensation,
A surprise, a shock.
A channel to funnel,
Ideas from this tunnel.
Dark corridors of thought,
Saying things we ought,
Not, but...

BLAH!

God! There it is again?
It's messin' with my zen!
But out it comes.
Shake it out,
Make a pout,
Verbal deluge,
Insanity interlude.
Wordy food,
In a crazy mood.
Patched into your mainframe,
Virtual is your pain game.
Feel it hit, the fast lane,
Insane in the membrane...

BLAH!

NOTHING THE SAME

Nothing seems to be the same,
No more.
The irony of my life,
Is a hole in the wall?
At a touch of a button,
Seals your fate.
Queuing down the alleyway,
They just can't wait.

Remember the fields,
Where we used to play ball?
Standing on the molehill,
Mountains seemed so small.
And life crawled past my window,
And scratched at my door.
It's a long time past,
Since time was threescore.

Nothin' seems the same,
No more.
Time passes like trains,
I was always off the rails.
Age came like a thief,
And stole my sails.

Remember the past,
In the present where it lives.
Memories are gifts,
That it always gives.
As now is so fleeting,
And the future, so raw.
Nothing is the same,
Nothing's the same,
No more.

OEUF

Two halves of a whole,
Two sides of a peg,
We are two sides,
Of the same egg.
Fit like a glove,
Robust like a keg,
We are two sides,
Of the same egg.
The curtain rises,
You whisper 'break a leg',
We are two sides,
Of the same egg.

OEUF

Two halves of a whole,
Two sides of a peg,
We are two sides,
Of the same egg.
Fit like a glove,
Robust like a keg,
We are two sides,
Of the same egg.
The curtain rises,
You whisper 'break a leg',
We are two sides,
Of the same egg.

LOVE'S LATENCY

There's a delay,
Between what you say,
And what I feel.
There's a sweet spot,
But I can't find it.
Dormant inside,
Guessing all the time.

Love's latency.
Can't seem to sync,
With the way you think.
Cagey all the time,
Should I just join the line?
Current flame in tow,
Always the last to know,
You.

Love's latency.
Do I just mime,
Save time,
Pretend the words are mix and match?
When the session's over,
Remember to detach.
With something this good,
There's always a catch.

Love's latency.
We seek soul synchronicity,
Honest simplicity.
Until we know our heart's frequency,
We can spend forever in inequality.
Saying our goodbyes,
Between the lines.

Love's latency.
Can't seem to sync,
With the way you think.
Cagey all the time,
Should I just join the line?
Current flame in tow,
Always the last to know,
You.

A PLACE TO BELONG

A place to belong,
Time to be strong,
A river to hide,
As new worlds collide.

Love can be like a house with many windows,
Or like a room with not one door.
Love can be like an attic with many cinders,
Or like a towering palace without a floor.

A place to belong,
Instincts can be wrong,
A time now to decide,
By which hand to abide.

We all have somewhere we belong,
But in destiny's confusion, we get it wrong.
We lose the reason and our seasons collide.
Without a friend who's on our side.

So you leave all your memories,
And chase the rising sun.
And the nearer you think you are,
The further you've become.
Nothing seems the same any more,
Those familiar faces,
Who now ignore,
What on earth are you living for?

A place to belong,
Time to be strong,
A river to hide,
As new worlds collide.

Who do you want to be?
Where do you want to go?
Living all this, living all that,
Why is it, you still don't know?
What really is your dream?
How do you let it grow?
Questions here, questions there
Can you let it show?

A place to belong,
Time to be strong,
You will find it too,
The place, is within you.

QUIET SOLACE

In the quiet solace of my mind,
I pause in time to reflect.
To see what great accomplishments or deeds,
I may have done, are doing, will do.
And I realise the reality, of my works,
For it is so true.
We are striving after wind,
An impatient mood, that drives us on.
But whilst in the fast lane of life,
Life itself passes us and is gone.
All the things I have done, are doing, will do.
I have not done, am not doing, I may not do,
Because time has run out.
Spent so much time running away,
Stopping is impossible today.

All I unsettle is dust.

All I make are tracks.

All I do is eighty on a good day.

THE PERFECT CADENCE

If this were the music of my heart,
What would be its tune?
Each note,
Would be a thought.
Each thought,
Would make a chord.
Each chord,
Would be a memory.
Each memory,
Would be a stave.

Each stave,
Would be a dream.
A place where memories,
And thoughts piece together.

A sharp,
Recollection.
Where our aspirations,
Fall flat.
Or our hopes,
Ascend.
Where we lay our burdens…

To rest.

PAIL FULL OF SORROW

I empty out my soul in a bucket,
Pail of tears to weigh me down.
I climb the hill and it feels like a mountain,
With all the waters welled inside.

Then I fall, words disperse like ashes,
I'm flayed across the printed page.
I splutter in a puddle,
So focused on this muddle,
I can't see the sunbeams from the shade.

I wade and wallow, pool full of trouble,
Drink the comfort of familiar strides.
Laying stranded, fish out of water,
Wondering why, the tears ran dry.

Now I stand, shaky and empty,
Pail of sorrow, so hollow now.
I walk the hill,
And with no sire of sorrow,
And the yoke that broke me,
Is lighter now.

Those tears that ran through crow's feet for gutters,
Have left disquieting thoughts behind.
Now I walk, tiptoe the ocean,
With no sadness, to eclipse my stride.

Pail full of sorrow,
Bucket full of grief.
When anguish steals me, like a thief.
Remind me now, it weighs me down,
Remind me not to, wear a frown.

And next time I have to carry,
A pail full of sorrow,
Remind me now, to put it down.
And each time I empty, my soul in a bucket,
To feel no shame to spill it out.

NEAR TO ME

I've met a man I truly love,
I want to fill these pages, with all the above.
Whilst my heart, is filled with joy,
This artful pen, I will employ.
To write a testament to my heart,
To log a miracle, from the start.
To find the shapes, to script my soul,
As I discover someone, who makes me whole.
Fisherman, I am your catch,
Gestated in passion, now love's hatch.
A fever consumes me that will not be bound,
I know I have found love, this time around.
Brightest stars, now hear my plea,
May he be forever,
Near to me.

TRISTE RICHE

Another long day,
Driving home in the rain.
Washes off my made-up face.
Of the quiet voice behind the nets,
Of forsaken dreams and past regrets.

Things I gave up,
For the mahogany dash.
For the fine polished life,
With the gabardine mishmash.

For the finer things I sold my soul,
These four walls surround my hole.
My nest of thorns, with sash windows and drape,
Shame it's a sham and the F&B is fake.

Now I sit vacant,
Surrounded by my mountains of things.
That fill the void.
Cushion the noise.
Of the pin drop you can hear,
When they say,
'She likes to be alone'.

THE NEW YEAR'S SONG

The New Year's 'ere,
The goose got fat.
Please spare ya pennies,
For the old man's hat.

Pass me a drink,
Pass me another.
The days when friends,
End up your lovers.

Under the influence,
Lift your restrain.
Do all the dares,
You'd n'ere entertain.

Last night of the year,
Two weeks to sign on.
What monotony,
What a fallacy,
What's the point, of goin' on?

D'ya know I paid taxes,
For the Queen and corgis.
I bet I got a share,
In those flash suits of Fergie's.

No longer part of the secular machine.
To be the realisation,
Of a computerised dream.

A machine took my job,
A machine took my pride.
Left with a valueless,
Empty hollow inside.

Slaved twenty years for the industrial fist,
What I got to show,
But a watch on my wrist.

The New Year's 'ere,
The goose got fat.
Please spare ya pennies,
For the old man's hat.

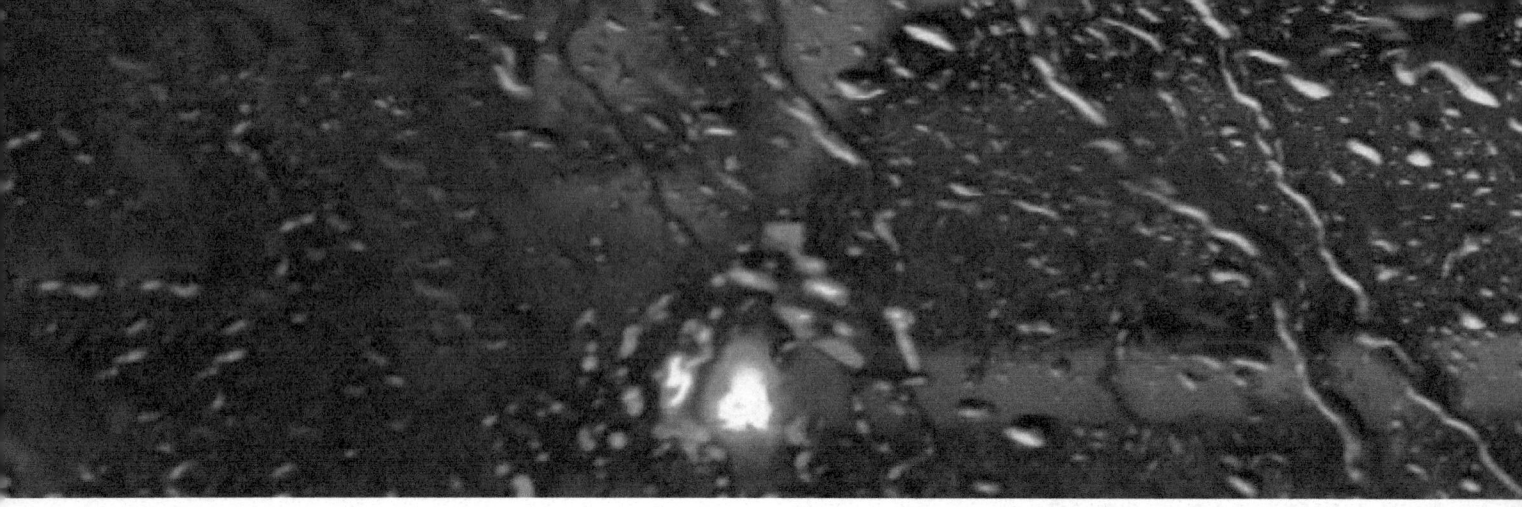

TAIL PLIGHT

The tail lights cast a shadow,
But the darkness hides my face,
The white lines hold me focused,
And I'm feeling my heart race.
I'm running away from the fool that I am,
When each leaf is opened I hear a door slam.
So I fear the confusion that comes with the strain,
I end all the chapters and slow down again.

Too much, too soon,
Why is life so short?
Why are dreams so long?
Why must you hurry, to the ending of the song.
Because his eyes did not want me,
And I knew something was wrong.
I could not touch it or feel it,
Or know what I had done.

But I thought it was me and I wanted to run,
To jump in my car and drive till the sun.
To jump in my car and drive far away,
From the flaky crazy woman in disarray.
To jump in my car and skid away the scars.
Rumble over the road rage and passing cars.
To watch the speedo shoot to the limit,
And race my heart, and I will forget it.

And I'll drive so hard,
Forget the nothing that I am,
You can wipe off the windscreen,
With a chamois leather hand.
Winter weather, ice and rain,
Washes out the pouring pain.
The tail lights cast a shadow,
The darkness hides my face.
Each request line pulls a bell cord,
Out peals my disgrace.

Ring road episode, nothing to feel.
Caught in the safety,
Of the wheel within a wheel.
A cycle of repetition,
Till there are no more fears.
Shiny eyes like spoons,
That scrape away the years.

The M25, heartbreak drive,
Round and round, I weep and weep,
But I'm still alive.
There's not a sound, cradled in my car,
Steering hard, flush against the tar.
Against the rage, nowt left to give,
A vacuum now, in which to live.
Bucket seats to drain it away,
The shadows are here, and here to stay.

The tail lights cast a shadow,
And the darkness is my face.
Shadows are my co-host,
In this crazy rat race.
Nothing but the road,
Caught in the catseyes,
In between the pretences,
And the liquor and lies.
Dial your dialling code,
As I hit the slip road.
Yearning now, to hear your voice,
Only turn is a dead-end choice.

No petrol in this tank,
No clever wit to thank.
Heater on full blast,
Whisks away the past.
I come to a halt, can taste the salt,
Of my dried-out tears, my crusted fears,
Driven too hard, for all these years.

My engine gently purrs,
A reassuring hum,
She tells me straight, to cut and run.
Shiny alloys, emotional noise,
Who needs to be, more than just boys' toys.
Wing mirrors in, silence the din,
No one to question, where you've been.
The tail lights cast a memory,
The darkness, is replaced.
The morning smells of promise,
And the shadows are erased.

STILLNESS

I am still.

Unaware, I'm holding my breath,
As you move closer and place a kiss on my mouth.
A burden that parts my lips, softens my clasp,
My lips moisten at the anticipation of your touch.
My barriers are breached, my resistance is futile,
I surrender my body in an eager embrace.
I close my eyes and open my thighs and I rise,
To catch my breath as it releases, in a long slow sigh.
I am water at your feet,
I am the ocean begging you to explore.
I feel the weight of your body,
Merging effortlessly with mine.
Entwined.
My body wraps around you like silk on skin,
Yearning to be within.
The moment,
As intense as just before a kiss,
The moment of bliss.
The urgent anticipation as you hover and swell,
Aching to connect,
So erect.
And so delectably edible in all ways,
I meet your gaze.
And slowly you slide, inside, passion is your guide,
I am your prey with nowhere to hide, I surrender.
My heart is still beating heavy like boots,
Thudding in my chest, my body is wet,
Beads of sweat, pour like rain, retain,
Like a leaf in a puddle, floating in the middle,
Nipples like nails,
Curtains blow like sails,
Our bodies merge into the darkness.

We are still.

BACK CONTENTS NEXT

SAD I

I make me sad sometimes.
I used to look up to myself,
Thought there was something there,
Worth fighting for.
Not sure, what more,
Is there,
Than there was before.
Anymore.

I make me sad sometimes.
Don't know what I'm doing here,
Wandered in from the dark.
Looking for a match,
To light my way,
That I lost before,
I lost what I was fighting for.
Don't know what's in store.
Anymore.

Tenses mingle and days merge.
Meaningless timeless string of balls,
Simultaneously unravelling,
But I don't know where.
Or what or how,
Or why I'm sad,
I only know it's me.
And I make me sad.
Sometimes.

I make me sad sometimes.
I don't want to be with me,
Why should anyone else's shoulder,
Need grazing,
From the sharp teeth of my bitter distrust.
What am I trying to find?
Someone else to give me the answers?
Someone else to take the blame?

I make me sad sometimes.
Because the simplest things perplex me,
The slightest hint of horizons,
And my body caves in.
Instant recall of immunity,
Maimed by the lightening,
Crippling disgust.
Of me.

I make me sad sometimes.
I see the difference in me,
The silence that follows me around,
Haunting my cave.

Average.
Common-or-garden,
Ten-to-the-dozen,
Pound for a pound.
Odd and unclear in a sea of sames.
Thought there was something more,
Than there was before, but if it was,
It's not there.
Anymore.

I make me sad sometimes.
But now it seems more than before,
Because I'm not a freak,
I'm just sick of picking up my own pieces.

I make me sad sometimes,
But I'm grateful it's only sometimes.

XMAS NEXTMASS

Nextmass ex-mass.
Pagan rites to party nights,
And shaggin' on knees,
Proliferating social disease.
And care not about the credit card bill,
The economic overspill.

Drink a lot.
Beat the wife,
Smile at Jonathan Ross on Xmas night.
Sway with the proletariat scum,
Kiss the dog, sleep in Pedigree Chum.
Spout out, the world by rote,
Ignore the ultimatum note.
Drown in, the western dream,
Ignore when you hear the children scream.
Catholic priests, kissing heads,
Bowing down to babies' beds.

Shoot them all.
Have done with rights,
Pagan rites to party fights.
Excuses for abuses,
To human rights.
To fairy lights.
Lost souls, with no way home,
The mother ship, the candy dip,
The children wait for Santa's trip.
Christ is Brian, the birthday boy,
Crucified for another toy.

Nextmass ex-mass.
Political correctness,
Free soup for the homeless.
Three hundred and sixty-four days,
Of couldn't care less.
Pagan rites to debauched nights,
Lay out the cookies,
Put out the lights.

Blissful ignorance, conscience clear,
Thank God it only comes but once a year.

X-Y

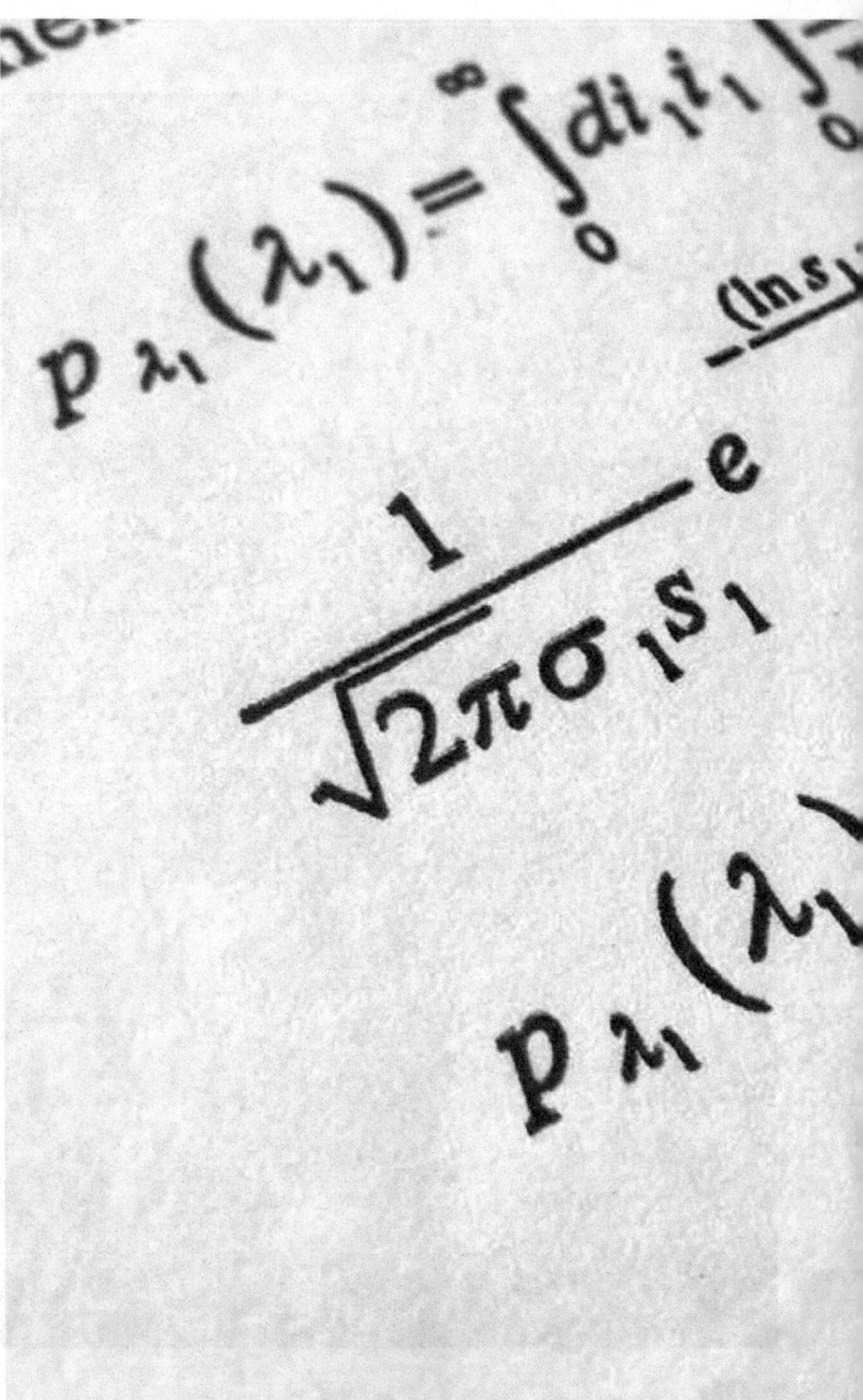

In the calculation you make,
I am a fraction.
In the world of passing,
I'm an attraction.
Just a blink,
No more.
When you're too busy,
You close the door.
I'm hanging and hanging,
I can't hold on anymore?

In the calculation you make,
I am a degree.
Whether to a greater or lesser extent,
We'll see.
Angles,
Obtuse,
Objective,
No use.
Busily subtracting and protracting,
But we don't add up to deuce.

In the calculation you make,
I am pi.
Need for meaning,
But you're never the Y.
Just a blink,
No more,
When you're too busy,
You close the door.
Keep your Y... now I'm your X,
Let's lay these opposites, to rest.

Time for goodbye...
To X and Y.

SYNC

I think we're in sync.
Special chink, favourite drink,
Bubbles and rum, our same time come.
Walks by the Thames, chocolate gems,
Scissor, paper, rock, the key to my lock.
The juice to my stock.
Eating wine gums, biting bums,
Hot cross bun fights, steamy nights,
Steamy texts, hot sex,
Fuzzy in my head, breakfast in bed.
Jacuzzi in the dark, perfect place to park,
Kissing my face, pounding drum and bass.
Beer and wine, breakfast line,
Clasping your hand, special duvet land.
Absorbed in calm, arm in arm,
Halves of a soul, go down the rabbit hole.
Sweating like junkies, dancing like monkeys,
At it like bunnies, bees to the honey.
I know and I think,
We are in sync.

APRIL SHOWERS

We all need a little rain.

A little rusty nail, to wash down the pain.
To grow miss sunshine, we need a little fame,
It gives us a reason, for an umbrella on the train.
To hold onto love, we need to find a way,
To find love, despite the rain.

Twenty-four hours, just one day.
The billboard went from red to grey,
And I thought I was so right, about what to say.
And I was stumped to the core,
The rusty nail left a bore,
In my heart and it fell, on the floor.
Any more rain and I would have clean washed away,
In twenty-four hours, just one day.

We all need a little rain.

They say when it rains it pours.
And I'm trying so hard, not to keep score.
Because even just knowing love for one day more,
In myself is worth it, even if we never find a way,
To find love, despite the rain.

Twenty-four hours, just one day.
I'm on my knees begging you to stay,
Foxhole believers, arm in arm we pray.
And so I keep, the nail in my heart,
The rusty nail, a love dart,
Stuck in my flesh, until the day we part.
Any more rain and I would have clean washed away,
In twenty-four hours, in just one day.

We all need a little rain.
As it washes clean, our life frame.
And when the mirror is clearer,
Our souls become dearer.
And we can find love, despite the rain.

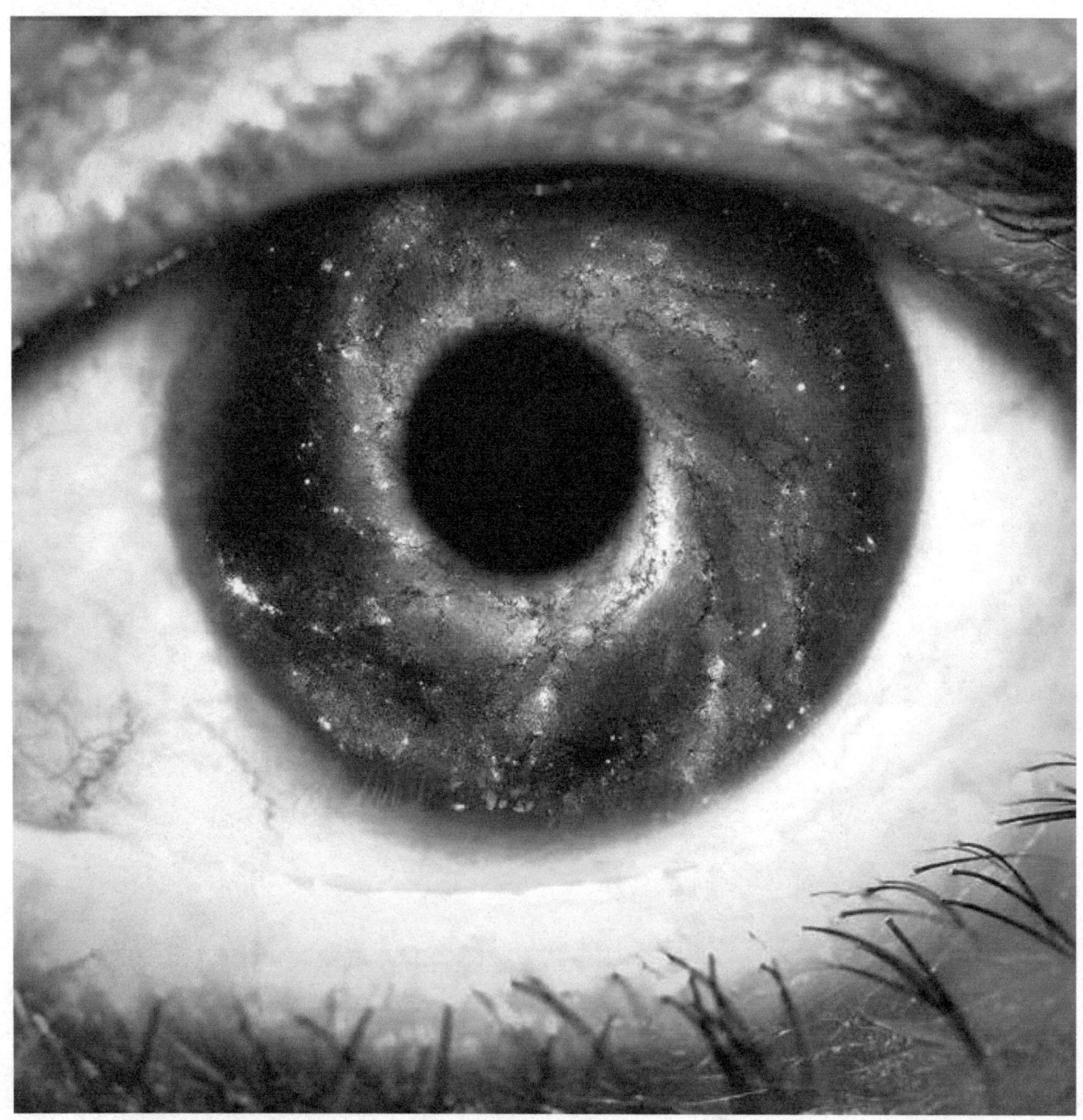

I AM THE UNIVERSE IN ME

I'm alive, I'm wired, I'm feeling inspired.
A new age has begun,
A new morning and a new sun.
And this new view has raised me higher,
And something new has stirred my fire.
Entering my heart dimension,
Lifted up again, by this soul ascension.
A secret knowing, that you're a mirror made by me.
At one, with the universe,
That is all there is to see.
Head inside of me,
And breathe in energy,
I feel the universe,
And the universe is in me.

And today I took the first step.
Today I stayed up the night,
And have not wept.
For I am the universe,
And I am never alone.
I am all my days today,
And the ache is outgrown.
And I know the air around me,
And anything is possible.
If I really let go,
I'm feeling so invincible.
Be the breeze,
Be the sea,
Be all the universe in me.

And love each moment as a chance to learn.
To seek your fire and let it burn.
And I am part of a new vibration,
Evolving higher to the next generation.

To the next illumination,
To the next visitation,
To a higher vibration,
To an energy generation.

I am the universe,
And the universe is in me.

BONSAI OF WORDS

To love unbounding,
Indulge in the resounding,
I taste these newfound nouns.
I chew at the bit,
I writhe and bite my lip,
I grind at the hip,
At the thought of these thoughts.
At the succour of these words,
Never heard,
Before, a closed door, a tight lid,
Saying things I never did.

And these taste so sweet,
There must be a warning,
A pumpkin at dawning.
Frantic, to chase the verb,
Before the kicking, to the kerb,
Gravity catches up with me,
Snaps me out from my fantasy,
I reach for word upon word, and up I scale,
Weaving vibrant verbs, into a fairy tale.

That's why I understand,
This moment was not planned.
And my conscious mind berates me still,
Of this, overwhelming will.
To write, insight, delight,
In the curves of words.
And the spaces between,
Like hertz in verse,
The bass reverbs.
In my paragraph autograph,
Graphic, like a photograph,
Reading like an epitaph.

If fate has a reason, I seek it still,
That's when my feelings overspill,
The words are like dross,
Skimmed off the top, and thrown aside,
Non-verbal chide.
I feel the loss,
Of my heart on a page,
A coming of age.
When you see the power,
In each thought, with a shape,
A gift in a whisper, whose offer to take.

So find awe in its power,
And don't read for my sake.
And know that what I seek,
This wisdom, words create.
Let it flow into the orchard of my mind,
And irrigate the soft fallows, of my skin,
To wash away the lacerations, from within.
And help this silent dreamer,
Find roots to begin.
Digging depths and dreaming dreams,
Immerse myself in verbal streams.

Tend and prune this bonsai of words,
Till something takes form,
In a shape to be heard.

I HAVE NO ANSWERS

There are no reasons,
And even less rhyme.
To the questions,
And conscience,
That plagues my mind.
Only that in life,
There are lines,
And cracks in the frame.
That perfection is fleeting,
Washes off like rain.

And whatever we seek,
Is not always meant, to be found.
And the riddles in philosophy,
Are the silence between the sound.
And nothing is simple,
Until we let it flow.
By forgetting the reasons,
And then letting it go.

And I have no answers,
Only the gentle bliss.
Of your unquestioning eyes,
And your subtle kiss.
So, one day,
I will break away.
And be worth more,
Than perfunctory.

And this is not an answer,
I have no answers.
This is just a quiet place,
Here in your arms.
A bus stop in life,
For temporary charms.
Am I the stop,
And you the greyhound,
Stop, unload,
And off without a sound.
Are you the stop?
And I'm the bus?

I arrive, you embark,
And I don't make a fuss?
In public at least,
Tabloid feast.

I'm sinking gently in your arms,
I'm thinking thoughts I can't explain.
And wondering if you feel the same,
Tired of playing this age-old game.
I know myself too,
And I want something from you.
Aside from just a space, in your bed,
Aside from just some room, in your head.

I'm not stupid, I'm not blind,
I'm too worn with care, to waste my time.
Yet I change like the wind,
I just want to be free.
Then there are days that I think,
Much more of me.
That I deserve fidelity.
Until then, I am free and untamed,
Wild and unnamed.
Until then, I am brazen and unashamed.

You know yourself too,
And I'm like a book, you just renew,
Have it to hand, when you're bored,
Sex in-between watching who scored.
You're not bothered, you're no defender,
You blatently have your own agenda.

Men are like prey to be caught,
Women are like fodder to be bought.
Marriage is like a graveyard of love,
Slip into routine like hand in glove.
In a flash, it's all gone,
The sweat's dry, the passion's quick-fried.
Fast food, not in the mood,
For love or talk, or warm loving gazes.
Two solitary bodies,
Take advantage, as the world ages.

Which is free with no binds,
No judging, nothing unkind.
Just life pure and simple.
There are no reasons,
And even less rhyme,
To the questions,
And conscience,
That plagues my mind.

Only that in life,
There are lines,
And cracks in the frame,
That perfection is fleeting,
And washes off like rain.
Last five minute wonder,
Then call it quits?
Because surely I deserve,
Much more than this?

COMMUTING MACHINE

All these people,
All these empty faces.
What are you staring at?
Feel the heat of the silent wordless air.

The clatter ticks our lives away,
Even our clothes fade to grey.
You tense like it was fate,
What drives you through this hell?

Over keen,
To be part of the machine.

A sea of dead faces,
Scuttling to their graves.
This sprawling overcrowded,
Mechanical, cynical metropolis.

Might as well find an adequate spot,
One assumes we'll be waiting here a lot.
Longer than you imagine it to be,
Trains seem to usually,
Do this kind of thing.

Bustling of mobile phones,
Checking out the ones at home.
Delayed again my dear so sorry,
Train seems to have hit a lorry.
Or something of that ilk,
Still, no use crying over spilt milk.
Pick your nails, adjust your tie,
Play Candy Crush, to pass the time by.
Crazy world, crazy people,
Come screaming on Sunday, from the steeple.

All these people,
All these empty faces.
What are you staring at?
Feel the heat of the silent wordless air.
Don't you ever urge to escape?
Where do you go?
Is it home to the prison,
Or to the studio?

Do you praise your achievement,
In the quiet of your gas fire lounge?
Who would notice if your space wasn't around?
That narrow little space you fill,
Between the platform and the train?

In those six minutes you save,
Compacted like sardines,
Do you dream of the ocean?

I'm sure people like you dream.
I'm like you,
I dream.

Turn on, tune in, suck up, cop out,
Don on the Fawkes, rise up and shout.
Breathe in each sigh and swallow your pride,
Take on the system, world order defied!
Fight for your freedom, for the right to decide,
Flush out the masons, so there's nowhere to hide.

Believe in the magic, that thoughts make things,
Trust in the truth and it will give you wings.
Dare to join the revolution,
Play your part in the global solution.
Embrace the rest of life with something more,
Than just a stifled chortle,
Over your latest Scrabble score.

All these people,
All these empty faces,
What are you staring at?
Feel the heat of the silent wordless air.
Who would notice if your space was empty?
That narrow little space you fill,
Between the platform and the train?

Dare to dream.
Commuting machine.

MUSIC IS

MUSIC IS emotions carried.
On waves of sound,
Vibrations,
That evoke and infuse,
A powerful consciousness.
To arouse and replenish.

MUSIC IS like a rainbow.
A multidimensional natural voice,
Communicating a spectrum of feeling,
In a unification of sound.
A oneness of thought.

MUSIC IS an unbiased expression.
In pure form it shows no prejudice,
Enjoyed by humankind,
Regardless of outward appearance.
A channel to peace.

MUSIC IS a weapon unparalleled.
Leading hearts to their grave,
Battlefields ring the funeral march,
Where they once called the flag of patriotism.
Music that never rang true.

MUSIC IS diverse like the universe.
Surviving the centuries,
Carrying and preserving history,
Teaching and learning each dawn.
Planting ideas and watching them grow.

MUSIC IS my undoing.
That shadows my reality,
That throws my heart to swine,
A pain that makes me inferior.
A train that always leaves early.

MUSIC IS my first love.
A joy I cannot explain,
An emotion I cannot score,
A feeling that excites me.
A cause I devote my life to.

MUSIC JUST IS.

START AGAIN

Stuck in this shopping queue,
Waiting to be the next in line.
So much of it is the wrong type of bread,
Rising in my head.
Seems the only way from wholemeal to plain,
Take it back and start again.

I'm out the door, short changed,
Wanting more from this than to be strange.
Weighed down with baggage in my brain,
Take it back and start again.

Walk to the shore twisted inside,
Wishing I could stop this tide.
The feeling that keeps welling up inside.
Restrain the inane,
Take it back and start again.

When half a minute is a lifetime,
I reach out for a lifeline.
But I've got nothing to hold it fast to,
No reason enough to do.
Just a whole pile of things,
For forensics to go through.

I'm sat alone as per usual,
Can't find a reason to move on to.
Just these silly words,
That keep me from the edge,
Drunk on life's ledge.

I'm back in the shopping queue,
Groundhog day,
Enough to eat, but still why stay?
My life could fill a thousand bags,
Dolce & Gabbana make good dishrags.

Take it back and start again,
This ache inside is a constant strain.
I have no fight left,
Feeling bereft.

But it's so funny that you care so much,
But can wipe it away in a single touch.
It is sad that you'll somehow, be in shock,
That when I go, you'll be half cocked.
And blown away by the blame,
Angry that I was selfish, in my pain.

Still stuck in the shopping queue,
Waiting next in line, for my time.
Who gives a toss if I'm whole but plain,
Take it back,
And start again.

WAITING

Waiting for your blessed touch,
Waiting and my hands are clutched.
Waiting my heart pounds in my chest,
Waiting and I cannot rest.
Waiting and my lips are wet,
Waiting and I can't forget.
Waiting for your blessed touch,
Waiting for the love, I love so much.
Waiting and my fingers press,
Waiting for the place, you know best.
Waiting and my lips are pursed,
Waiting for you to quench my thirst.
Waiting and minutes feel like hours,
Waiting for the scent of flowers.
Waiting I can wait no more,
Waiting then you knock at my door.

TREASURE BOX

I put all our treasures, in a box,
All the party ribbons and the random rocks.
And stones with holes and a broken shell,
Incidentals of farewell.

I put all our treasures safe, and closed the lid,
And cried for the memories, like a lost kid.
All the rave tickets and the concert bands,
The hotel keys and wedding plans.

I put all our treasures, away for good.
I wish this fairy tale, had gone the way it should.
The valentine cards and the Christmas wish,
My heart can't stomach, this bitter dish.

I put all our treasures, away for safe keeping,
And stuck it up with tape, to stop the memories from seeping.
But I can't let it go, and I can't close the box,
So I take one last look, at the random rocks.

I put all our treasures deep in my heart.
And will keepsake the good times, we had at the start.
Now it's time, to box up and move on.
And find new treasures,
And write,
A new song.

I AM MY DREAMS

I am a quiet dreamer,
I sail the ocean of my dreams.
I wonder, what's the meaning,
Of this foolish pipe dream.
Each day is not enough,
There seems so much more to learn.
I wonder, what's the reason why,
I hesitate at every turn?

Sometimes I have no hand to hold,
No rock to make me strong.
And when I feel alone, and lost,
And I know I can't go on.

I breathe love to my soul,
Universal energy makes me whole.
I hold my heart in my hand,
You give me strength to make a stand.
I become the ocean,
And then I am my dreams.

The universe can open your heart,
With just one line.
If you dare to dream your dreams,
You are a step nearer divine.

Merge in the water.
Be a cosmic aorta,
And your truth will easily flow.

My gift to me,
Is energy,
And now I live,
I am my dreams.

Hey don't think for a moment,
I'm not saying that I'm perfect.
There's so many issue rivers, left to cross.
I get days of regression,
I fall back into depression,
And I feel like my dream's a lost cause.

When friendship frays,
With darker days,
And you can't see your North Star.
Don't let the subtle kicks,
From the hypocrites,
Stop you from being who you are.
But the lesson is,
To continue to be.
Nod your mind, in time,
And then fly free.

So to you soul sailors,
Do yourself a big favour,
And don't stop believing in your goals.
Just flow with the motion in the ocean,
And cause a commotion,
Let the universe feed your soul.

Sometimes I have no hand to hold,
No rock to make me strong.
And when I feel alone, and lost,
And I know I can't go on.

I breathe love to my soul,
Universal energy makes me whole.
I hold my heart, in my hand,
You give me strength to make a stand.
I become the ocean,
And then,
I am my dreams.

TOLERANCE

Listen to the silence,
Breath of ignorance,
Death holds no banner,
Hollow voice piled high.

Issues,
Distant voices,
Angered spirits,
Deafened and defeated,
Ignorance in phase with apathy.

Unresolved,
Weighty chalice,
Filled with unrest,
Brimming with,
Unwillingness.

Injustice,
Patter in the storm,
Echo is lost,
Statues of lifeless ignorance.

Eyes,
Windows to the soul,
Tainted with time,
Painted with façade.

Equality,
Repression wears black,
Aggression wears red,
Tolerance wears thin.

A YEAR

A year of troubles,
A year of stress,
A year of heartache,
A year of mess.
A year of adventure,
A year of shmoo,
A year of blessings,
A year of you.
A year of laughter,
A year of sex,
A year of happiness,
A year of, what's next?
A year of music,
A year of beats,
A year of bass,
A year of repeats.
A year of sighs,
A year of learning,
A year of testing,
A year of burning.
A year of time,
A year of age,
Now it's time,
For a new page.

Want another copy of this book?
A poem of your own?
Or to find out more about the author?

Visit www.morgansheridan.com
or email morgansheridan@me.com

INTERNAL ANGLES

© 2024 Morgan Ellia Sheridan. All rights reserved. ISBN 978-0-9956946-0-6